ON MARTHA'S VINEYARD

Watercolor Impressions
by Robert L. Bowden

UNIVERSE

First published in the United States of America in 2003
by UNIVERSE PUBLISHING
A Division of Rizzoli International Publications, Inc.
300 Park Avenue South
New York, NY 10010

2003 2004 2005 2006 2007 / 10 9 8 7 6 5 4 3 2 1

Printed in Belgium

ISBN: 0-7893-0878-9

Library of Congress Control Number: 2002115766

ACKNOWLEDGMENTS

My thanks and appreciation to John Roberts
for his guidance in the reproduction of my
art; Nancy Hanst, who managed the pitfalls
of text; Kevin and Barbara Butler, who
initiated the Martha's Vineyard watercolors
and encouraged production of this book; and
to Mason and Gil Walsh and Mike and Sara
Shannon for their generous hospitality.
Special thanks to John Brancati and Charles
Miers at Rizzoli/Universe. Much gratitude to
my editor, Jessica Fuller, whose patience
and attention to detail produced a cohesive
account of my summer visits to Martha's
Vineyard. And need I mention, Diana.

Front jacket:
THE READING ROOM AND INNER HARBOR
2002, watercolor, 17$\frac{1}{8}$" x 23$\frac{1}{4}$"

Front end paper:
BELOW GAY HEAD CLIFFS
2002, watercolor, 11" x 16$\frac{1}{2}$"

MARTHA'S VINEYARD

West Chop

East Chop

Tisbury

Nantucket Sound

Vineyard Sound

Oak Bluffs

N

W — E

S

West Tisbury

Edgartown

Chilmark

Choppaquiddick Is.

Menemsha

Aquinnah
(Gay Head)

Atlantic Ocean

Introduction

I really came to know Martha's Vineyard when I was asked to exhibit my watercolors at a gallery in Edgartown. I took this opportunity to explore this large beautiful island, with its variety of landscapes, seascapes, and small towns. From the spectacular colored cliffs of Aquinnah to the solitude of Chappaquidick, I found far more to contemplate and paint than time allowed; these places are all about natural beauty. Then there are also the fishing communities—especially Menemsha, rugged and weathered, a hub of commercial fishing that evokes an older Martha's Vineyard. Sedate Edgartown is the home of sailing and boating enthusiasts, and it bustles with shoppers and sightseers. With its dignified Captain's houses and manicured neighborhoods, it looks nothing like Oak Bluffs—a community with multicolored, whimsical gingerbread houses. West Tisbury offers yet another entirely different environment of small farms, grazing cattle and sheep, elegant horse farms, and ponds. In Chilmark, my favorite, I found rolling hills, secluded houses, untamed natural forms, and splendid water vistas. All of these furnished a wealth of subjects to paint.

I began painting watercolors some thirty-five years ago. The watercolor medium is immediate, challenging, and easily transportable. It is comfortable to paint outdoors, whether the day is gray or sunny, or the temperature is hot or coolish. When I happen upon a subject that is promising I know it at once. I see the composition in my mind's eye. It takes only a few minutes to set up the easel, lay out the materials, and begin the drawing that evolves into the painting.

So there I was, set up to paint on the dock at Edgartown Harbor. It was a coolish, blustery day in June. Whoosh-water from a boatman's hose accidently swept across my painting. Another day, after several hours of painting, I was chased from a private property that was not marked as such. But these were not insurmountable problems. The myriad of sights and sites on Martha's Vineyard provided endless inspiration. The subjects were a gigantic tree, several cows in a pasture, a clammer foraging for dinner, an ornate house, men gathering their gear to go fishing, or a lonely beach.

And so it was on Martha's Vineyard, where I found the formal and the funky; the composed and the wild; commerce and recreation; solitude and activity. Its healthy pulse and continuous rhythm can be felt as one gets to know it.

—Robert L. Bowden

When painting on site, out-of-doors,
one should be ready for anything.
In this instance I received a brief shower
from a nearby fisherman as he was hosing
out his boat. He was very apologetic.

5. Houses on Morse Street
2002, watercolor, 17" x 23"

Fenced yards, well-manicured
gardens, sidewalks . . . a
long-established neighborhood
that barely hints at the nearby harbor.

Discovering that *"dead end"*
doesn't always mean "don't go there."

S*tark simplicity contrasts with a neighborhood of warm and inviting homes.*

13

This open harbor, painted in June,
was packed with all shapes
and sizes of watercraft
when I returned in August.

One of my favorite painting sites
on the Vineyard. Weathered colors,
textures, and shapes are everywhere.

17

10. Diana at Wasque Point, Chappaquiddick
2002, watercolor, 15" x 22"

This day's definition of serenity
is Wasque Point on Chappaquiddick Island.

18

An Edgartown Street
looks like a watercolor.

The beautiful schooner in the foreground is
the WHEN AND IF. On the day I painted her, I
didn't know her name or history. She was built
for General George S. Patton in the 1930s
and was to take the Pattons on a world cruise.
However, General Patton did not return
from Germany. In the 1990s, she was rebuilt
and upgraded by Gannon and Benjamin
of Vineyard Haven, who now manage her
for charter.

The road begins in a residential part of Edgartown.
When I followed it, I discovered
the inspiration for its name.

We drove to Menemsha to buy fresh fish
for dinner. While Diana was in
Larson's, I began this composition of a
docked fishing boat's complicated
rigging and machinery, other boats across
the channel, and the distant hills.
Adding to the challenge was the fierce,
blustery wind. I had to anchor the paper
with my free hand.

A delight . . . housewares, groceries, produce,
hardware, videos, ATM, post office, and
the list goes on. If they don't have it,
you don't need it. And there are
chairs on the porch to
encourage lingering.

ALLEY'S
General Store

Robert E. Bowden 10/02

Fishing and black dog,
two essentials of Martha's Vineyard.

The sign still reads School,
*but this building is now a library.
Appropriately, Diana is reading
while I paint.*

33

Quiet October morning.
The grazing cows were cooperative
in their slow movement
around the pasture.

Horizontals and verticals are
*accented in the afternoon light.
And it's a home, too.*

37

20. From South Abel's Hill facing Chilmark Pond
2002, watercolor, 50½" x 15½"

*L*ate afternoon light intensifies the foliage colors
and causes the bodies of water
to contrast light and dark.

An early morning excursion
with a fellow painter.
Nearby, several cyclists wait
for the bikes-only ferry.

22. SUNRISE AT OCEAN PARK IN OAK BLUFFS
2002, watercolor, 8 3/4" x 12 1/4"

A few early risers
enjoy the quiet and the view
of Nantucket Sound.

Long time fishing buddies,
Chris and Mike, prepare to make
their catch of the day
from Chappy's East Beach.
A four-wheel-drive vehicle equipped
with the indispensible rod holder,
fishing rods, and other extensive fishing
gear—the essentials for the
island fisherman.

Ⅰn 1880, it was known as "Tabernacle City" or "Cottage City" because it was a meeting place for prayer and reflection. In 1907, it was renamed Oak Bluffs. Since there was no whaling or shipping here, it became the island's first summer resort. The multicolored gingerbread houses that sprung up back then remain, and lend the town its present funky look.

25. LAKE AVENUE HOUSE
2002, watercolor, 6³/₄" x 10¹/₄"

46

No longer a traditional church,
it is owned by the Martha's Vineyard
Preservation Trust. The old
whaling church is now a place
for town meetings, concerts,
lectures, memorial services, and
weddings. Our friends were
married here eighteen years ago.

The famous Black Dog.
Is there anything more to be said?

The summer reunion.
Cousins and friends play
near Arruda Point
on Chappaquiddick.

Near *Music Street, this graceful porch
architecture caught my eye on
a quiet Sunday afternoon.*

Many artists are fascinated
by the tortuous limbs of this oak tree,
reputed to be the oldest on the Vineyard.
I was told Alfred Eisenstadt photographed it.

While I was painting, a tour of
photographers stopped to capture this
typical New England church,
shooting it from every angle.

A *clammer scours the shallow waters
hoping to find enough bounty for dinner.
A noisy heron watched for thirty minutes
or so while I painted.*

Autumn crowds gone, temperature
moderate, sky filmy blue, and
hardly any activity passing by as
I paint from a porch of
a closed up Victorian house.

LIST OF WATERCOLORS

1. THE READING ROOM AND INNER HARBOR. 2002, watercolor, 17$\frac{1}{8}$" x 23$\frac{1}{4}$" jacket, front
2. BELOW GAY HEAD CLIFFS. 2002, watercolor, 11" x 16$\frac{1}{2}$" (detail)
3. HOUSE ON NORTH WATER STREET. 2002, watercolor, 16" x 22"
4. EDGARTOWN INNER HARBOR. 2002, watercolor, 10$\frac{3}{4}$" x 14$\frac{7}{8}$"
5. HOUSES ON MORSE STREET. 2002, watercolor, 17" x 23"
6. BY BUTLER'S MUDHOLE AT EEL POND, EDGARTOWN. 2002, watercolor, 17" x 23"
7. WEST CHOP LIGHTHOUSE. 2002, watercolor, 11$\frac{1}{4}$" x 14$\frac{1}{2}$"
8. OAK BLUFFS HARBOR. 2002, watercolor, 17$\frac{3}{4}$" x 22$\frac{5}{8}$"
9. FISHING SHACK, MENEMSHA. 2002, watercolor, 10$\frac{3}{4}$" x 13"
10. DIANA AT WASQUE POINT, CHAPPAQUIDDICK. 2002, watercolor, 15" x 22"
11. SCHOOL STREET, EDGARTOWN. 2002, watercolor, 11$\frac{1}{4}$" x 15$\frac{1}{2}$"
12. THE WHEN AND IF, ALABAMA, AND ISLANDER. 2002, watercolor, 15" x 21$\frac{1}{4}$"
13. MEADOW OFF PLANTING FIELD WAY. 2002, watercolor, 16$\frac{7}{8}$" x 22$\frac{7}{8}$"
14. THE MARY ANN AND VERNA AT DUTCHER DOCK. 2002, watercolor, 10$\frac{1}{2}$" x 14"
15. ALLEY'S GENERAL STORE, WEST TISBURY. 2002, watercolor, 10$\frac{1}{2}$" x 16$\frac{3}{4}$"
16. ON THE JETTY AT CAPE POGE, CHAPPAQUIDDICK. 2002, watercolor, 10" x 14$\frac{1}{2}$" (detail)
17. MENEMSHA SCHOOL. 2002, watercolor, 9$\frac{3}{4}$" x 12$\frac{7}{8}$"
18. NIP AND TUCK FARM, NORTH TISBURY. 2002, watercolor, 9$\frac{1}{4}$" x 14"
19. 85 SOUTH SUMMER STREET, EDGARTOWN. 2002, watercolor, 17" x 23"
20. FROM SOUTH ABEL'S HILL FACING CHILMARK POND. 2002, watercolor, 5$\frac{1}{2}$" x 15$\frac{1}{2}$"
21. CRANBERRY LANDS, MENEMSHA. 2002, watercolor, 9$\frac{1}{4}$" x 12$\frac{5}{8}$"
22. SUNRISE AT OCEAN PARK IN OAK BLUFFS. 2002, watercolor, 8$\frac{3}{4}$" x 12$\frac{1}{4}$"
23. OLD FRIENDS. 2002, watercolor, 5$\frac{3}{4}$" x 8$\frac{1}{4}$"
24. HOUSE ON OCEAN AVENUE. 2002, watercolor, 6" x 9"
25. LAKE AVENUE HOUSE. 2002, watercolor, 6$\frac{3}{4}$" x 10$\frac{1}{4}$"
26. THE OLD WHALING CHURCH. 2002, watercolor, 8$\frac{3}{4}$" x 14"
27. THE BLACK DOG TAVERN. 2002, watercolor, 16$\frac{1}{2}$" x 10$\frac{1}{2}$"
28. GRANDCHILDREN AT THE BEACH. 2002, watercolor, 6$\frac{1}{2}$" x 11"
29. HOUSE ON SOUTH ROAD, WEST TISBURY. 2002, watercolor, 10$\frac{1}{4}$" x 15"
30. THE LANDMARK TREE. 2002, watercolor, 10$\frac{1}{2}$" x 15"
31. FIRST CONGREGATIONAL CHURCH. 2002, watercolor, 11" x 17$\frac{1}{8}$"
32. LATE AFTERNOON AT NASHAQUITSA POND. 2002, watercolor, 11" x 16$\frac{1}{2}$"
33. FROM CHOP HOUSE, EAST CHOP. 2002, watercolor, 11$\frac{1}{4}$" x 16$\frac{3}{4}$"
34. FLOWER STAND. 2002, watercolor, 10" x 6"
35. ON PHILBIN BEACH, LOOKING SOUTHEAST, AQUINNAH. 2002, watercolor, 11" x 16$\frac{1}{2}$" (detail)
36. FARMER'S MARKET DISPLAY. 2002, watercolor, 8" x 8" on jacket, back

34. FLOWER STAND
2002, watercolor, 10" x 6"

FOLLOWING PAGES:
35. ON PHILBIN BEACH,
LOOKING SOUTHEAST, AQUINNAH
2002, watercolor, 11" x 16$\frac{1}{2}$"